DENDRITES

JAY SNODGRASS

2 0 1 5

Hysterical Books
Tallahassee, FL Thomasville, GA

ISBN 978-1508922124

for Kristine

I've been here, near you
in the water,
where everything breaks upon.

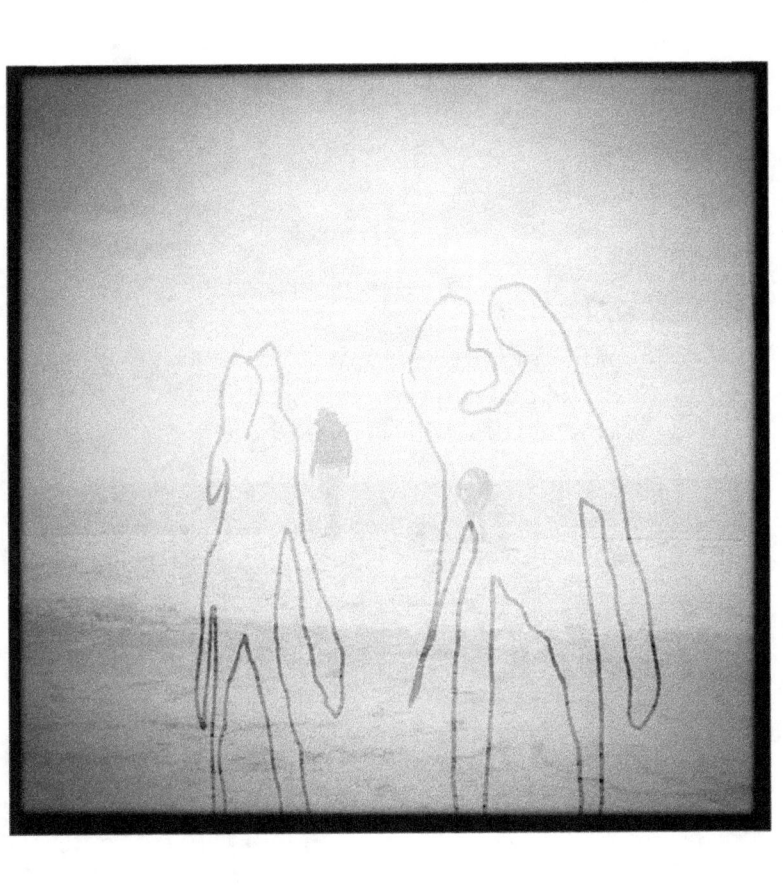

Sometimes the trees never come back
after you've taken their fruit.
Why would they, with all these people?

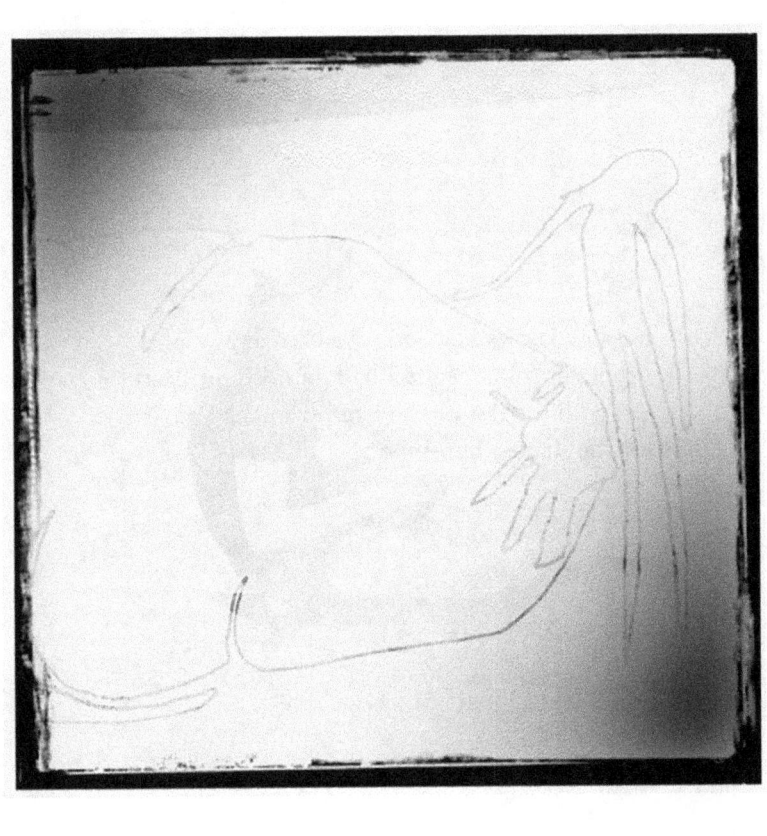

No one knows how long I've been away.
I thought for a second I had dumped my heart
out with the rest of the ashtray. Thank you
for the shape I remember.

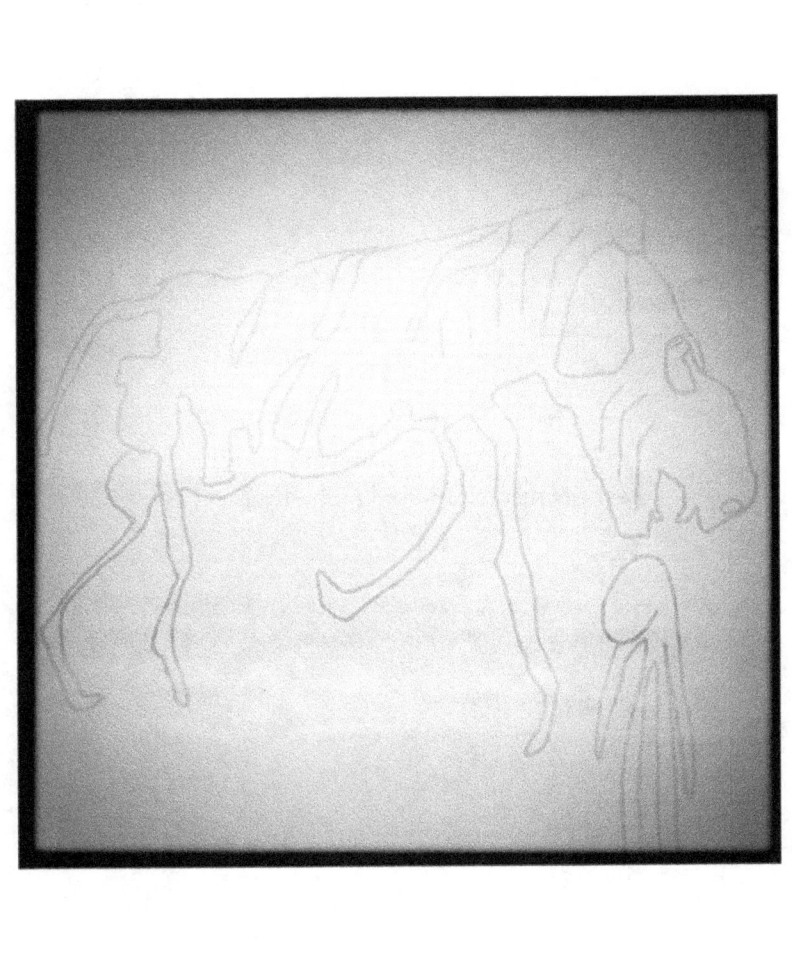

Someone drops a brick on the street.
It's late. I look at the hammer I hung up
over the mantel. Bruised monument.

MAR 85

Birds speak to the morning
sidewalk, No one knows.
I feel the air turn dark
again.

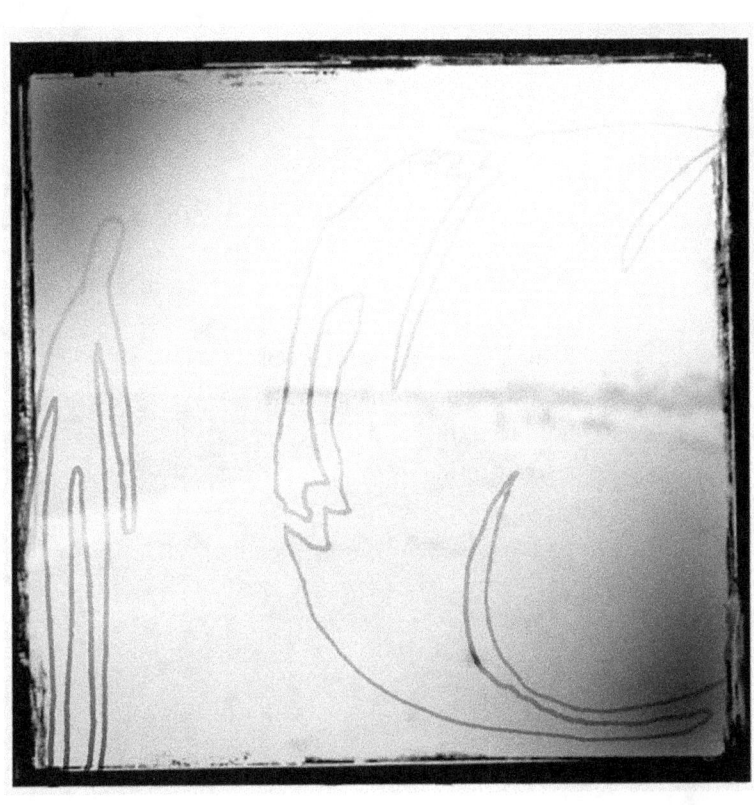

I think about the sand. Look
at a printout of the universe,
hold it in my hand. It has
a secret taste.

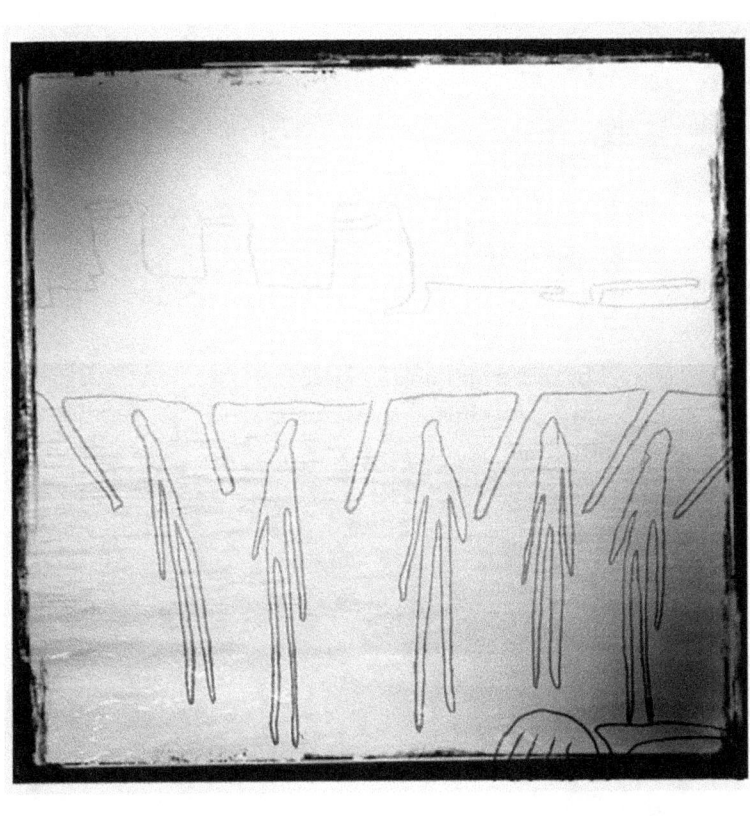

The ocean and bread. Succor
and a sandwhich. Day is the presence
of a star.

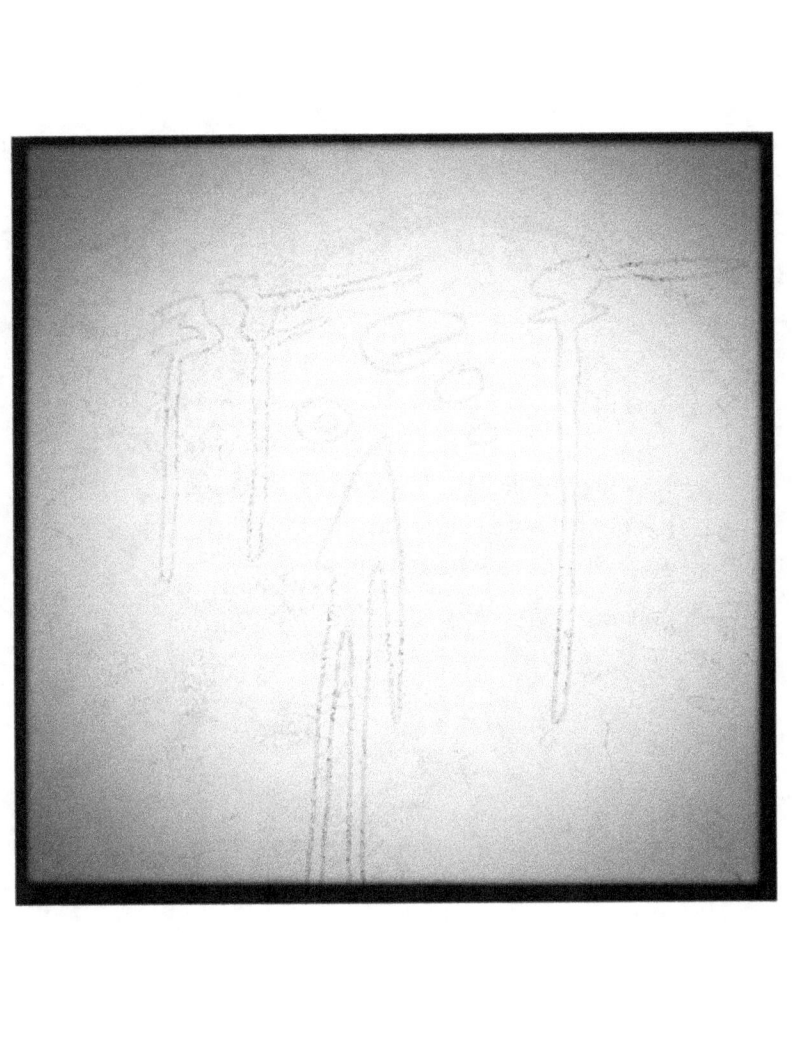

It seems like the leaves take even longer to fall now, longer than the morning. Now everything is strange.

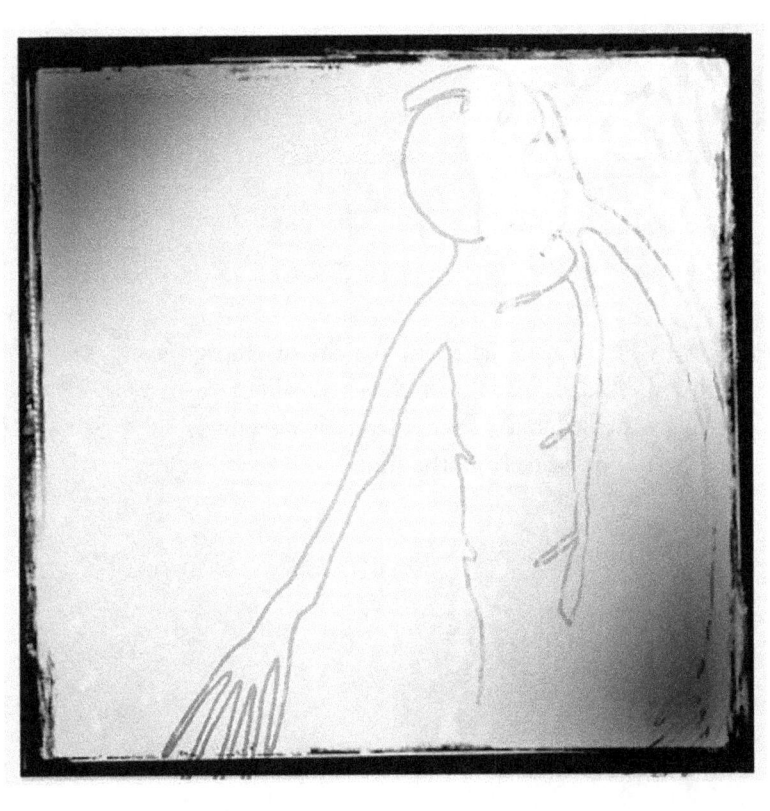

I'm in a special room in a city of empty glasses.
All of it made from the sheer will of cigarettes
formed, like a friend, from dying winter,
signaled to from the shore.

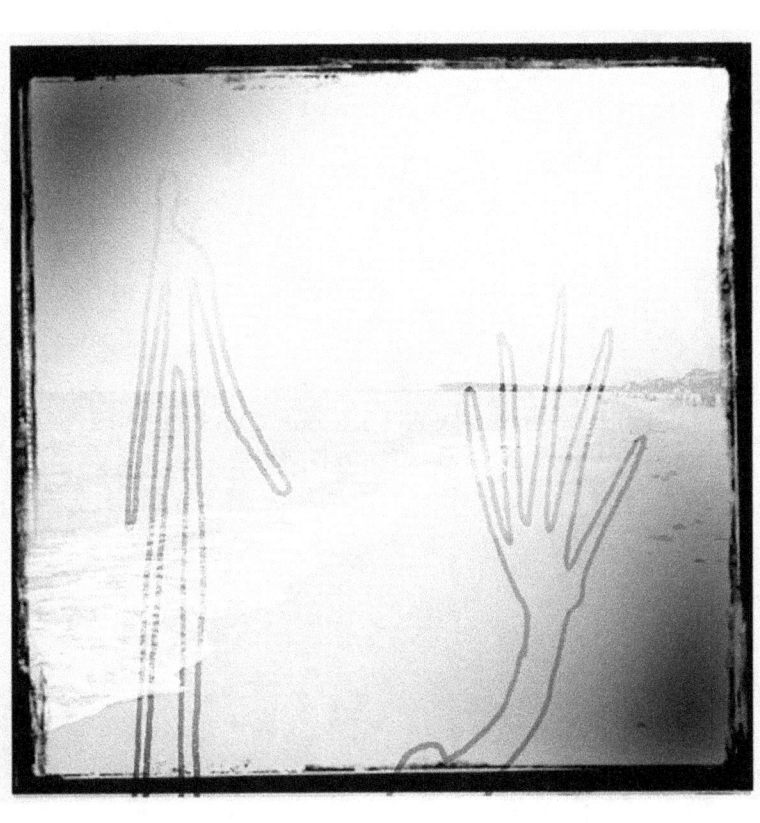

I do feel bad for plants in early spring,
so much waiting and cold birds, puffed and turning
together away in disappointment.

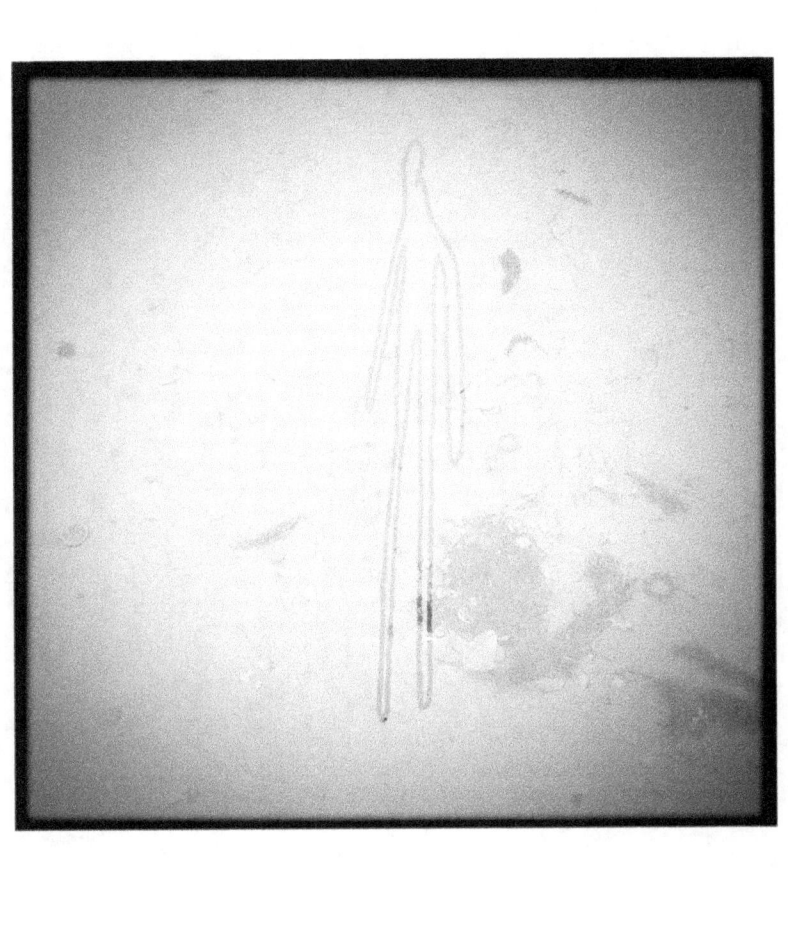

The priest with two heads toasts
this glass of light, he is not my real father
who is a storm at sea, roiling
beneath the stars.

Sometimes you are late, running.
This is not a dream. Keep breathing,
it will end.

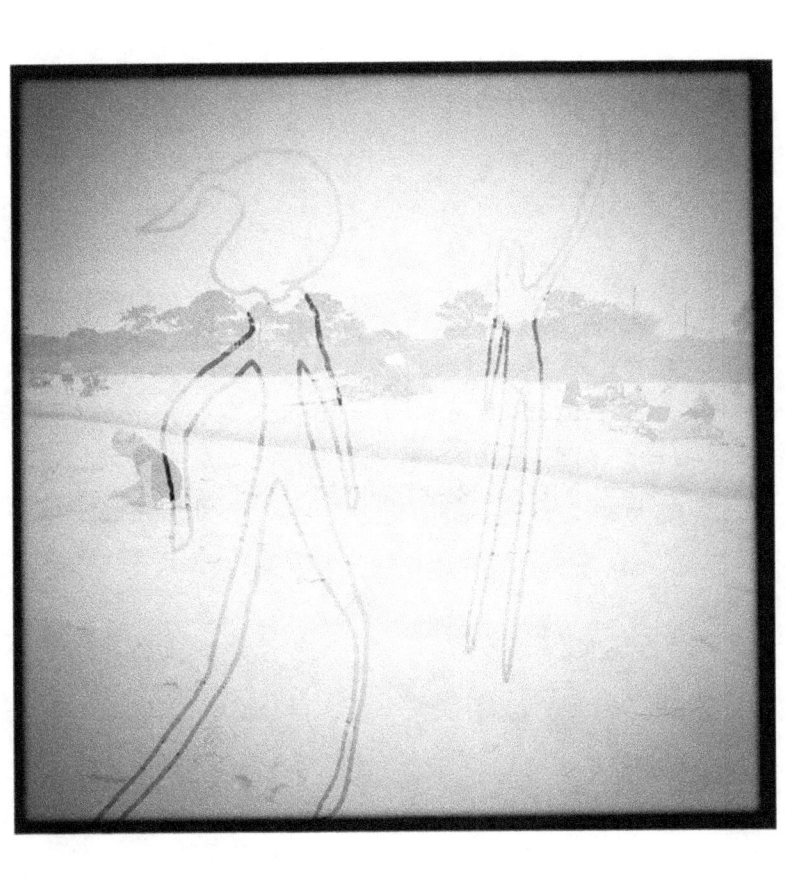

Roadside of lines, liniments,
pecan groves, citrus tongues,
fortified against mouths.

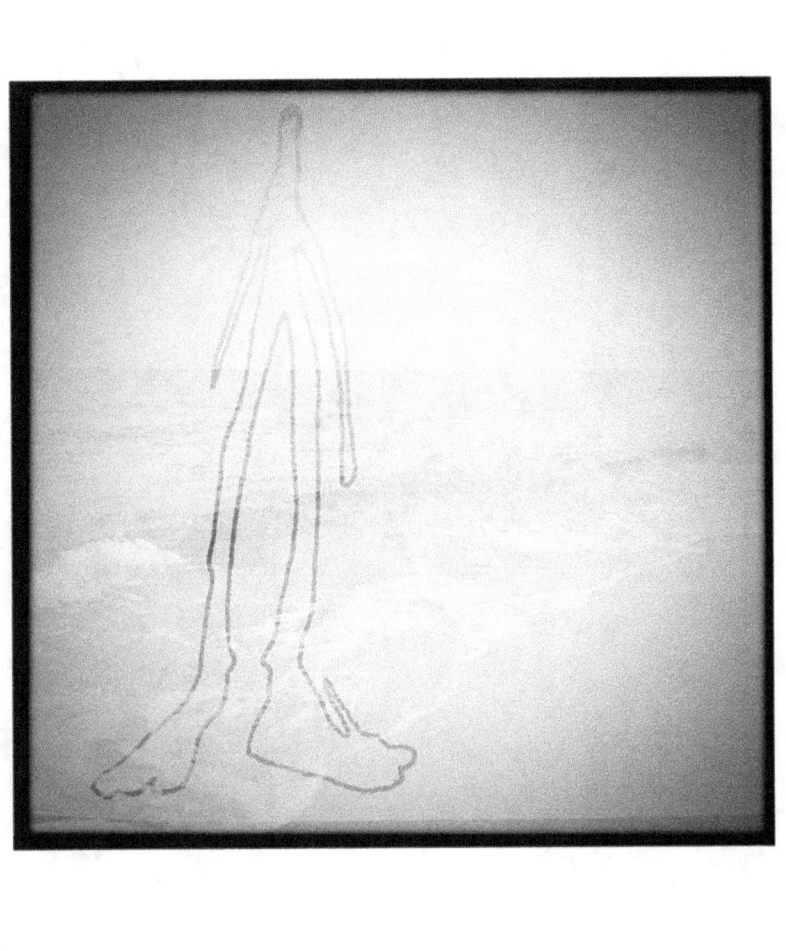

Smiles are brought to life
the way fruit is, with time
and a knife. So much laughter
in heaven.

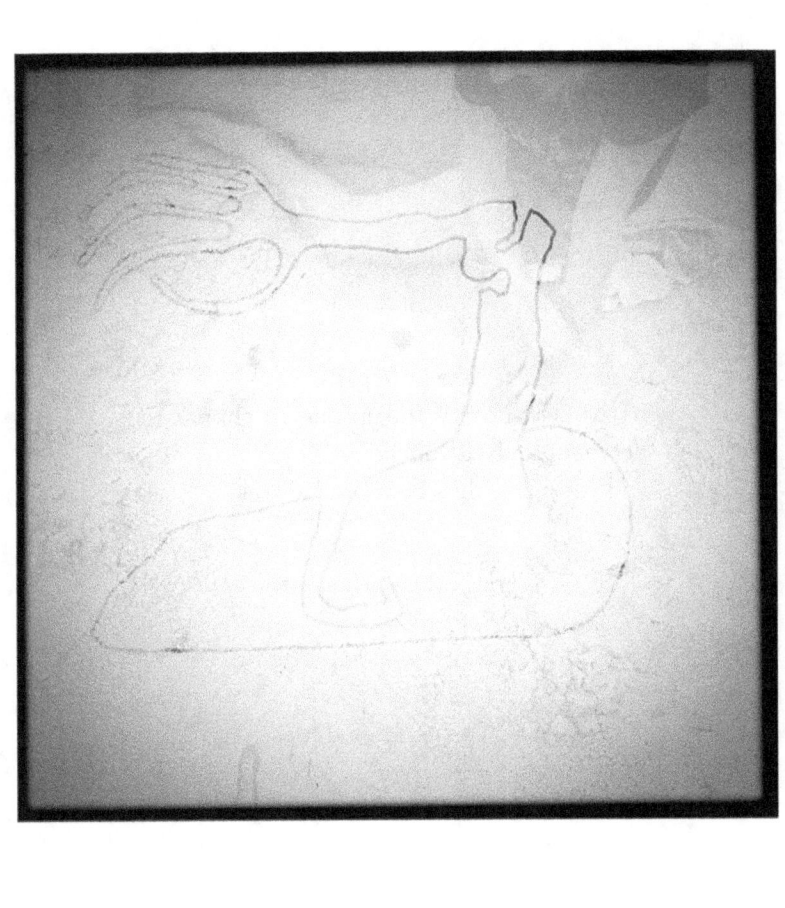

These pills are like little pads
to the kickdrum of the upstairs neighbor's
heavy footfalls. Dandelions
and whispers. She's been dead a weak.

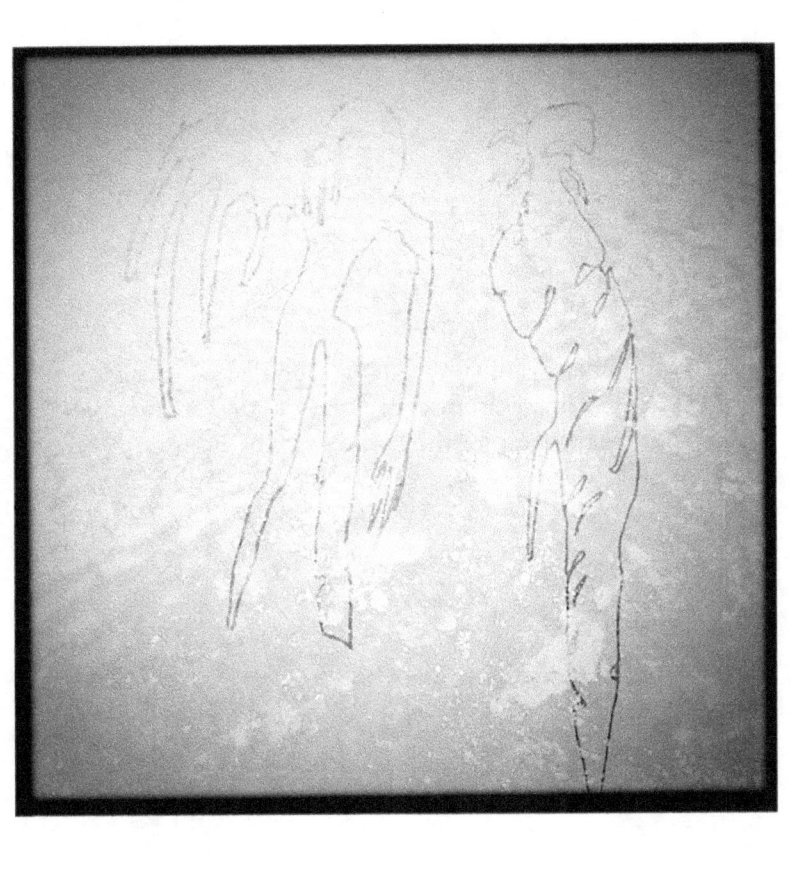

They've buried the phone lines
like desires, sutures of light waiting
in the dark for the TV to come back.

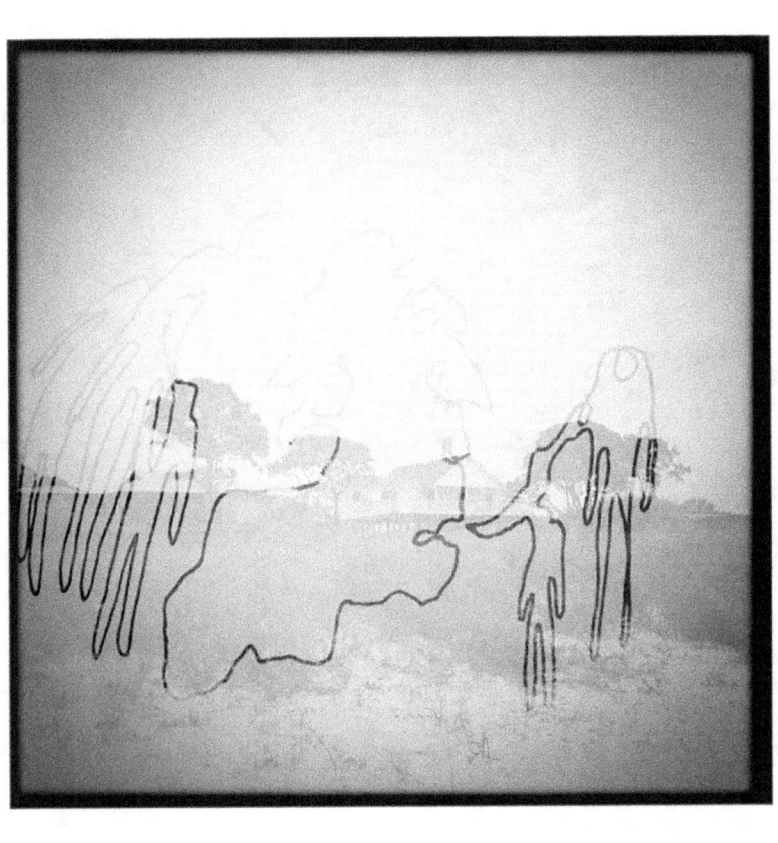

Just above the alter a pulse
of light hovers over the rooftops
like psychic wingbeats.

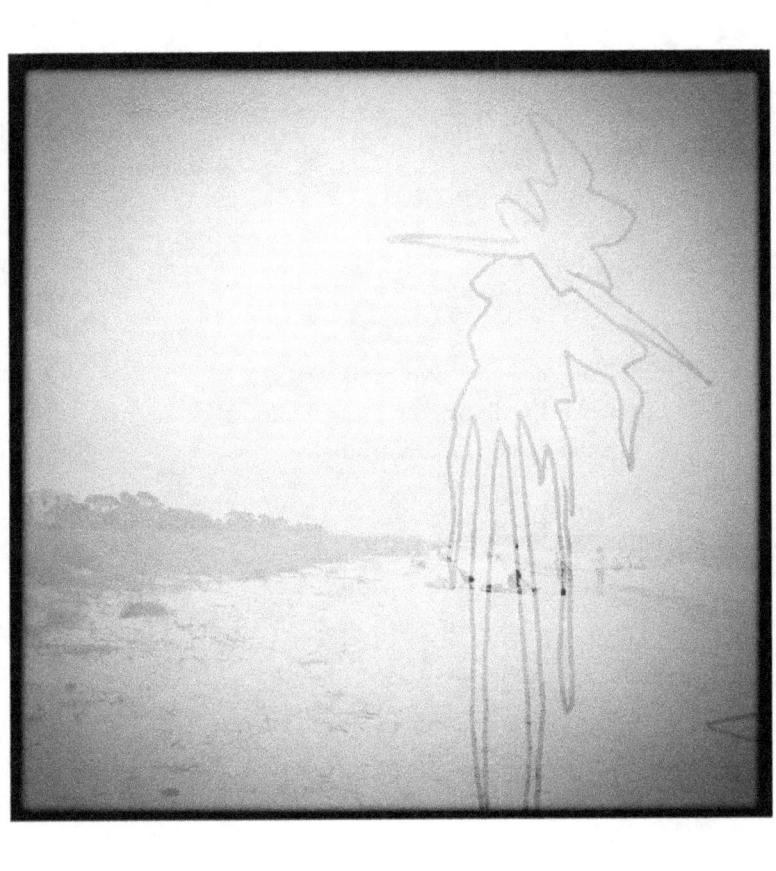

Tiny layers of skin break off
when I walk or shave. fragile motes,
radiant snowfall, returning.

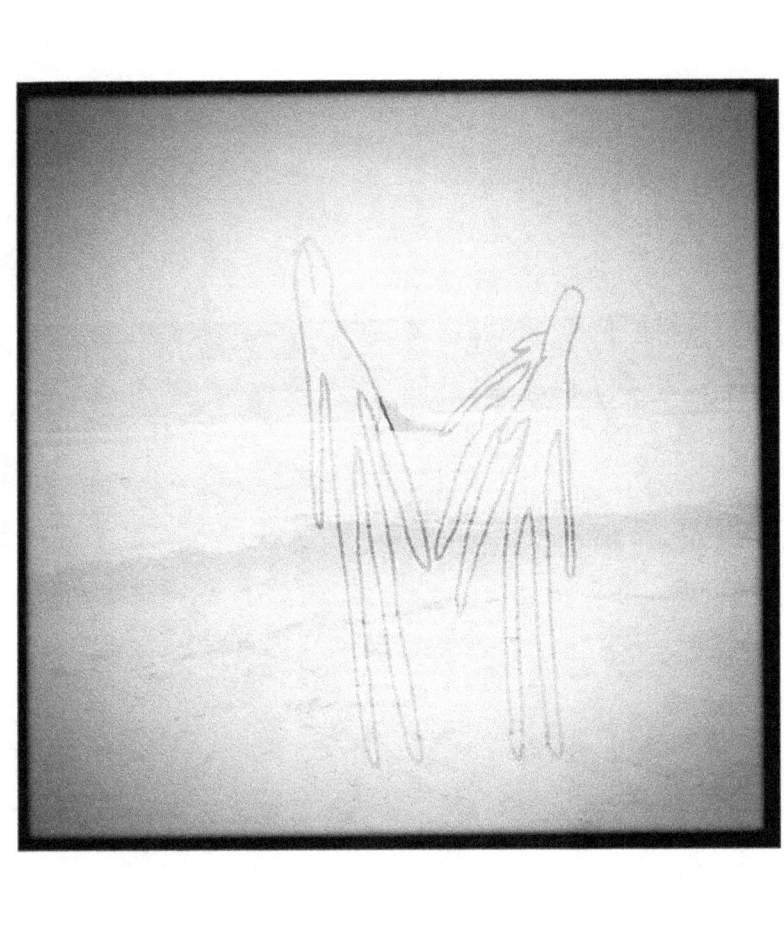

I followed a lie
down to the water's edge
where I was supposed to let go
of childhood's dark
hair and let him drown.

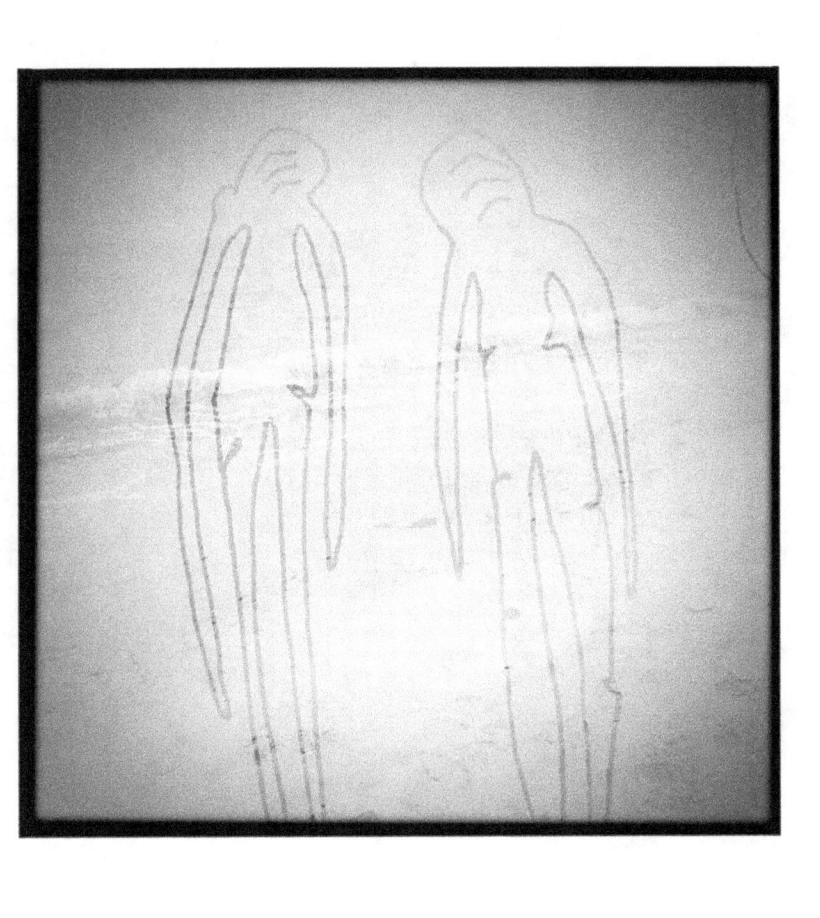

Out there, the faces in the grate,
are partying with their own ghosts.
I'm a candle, lit for its submergence.

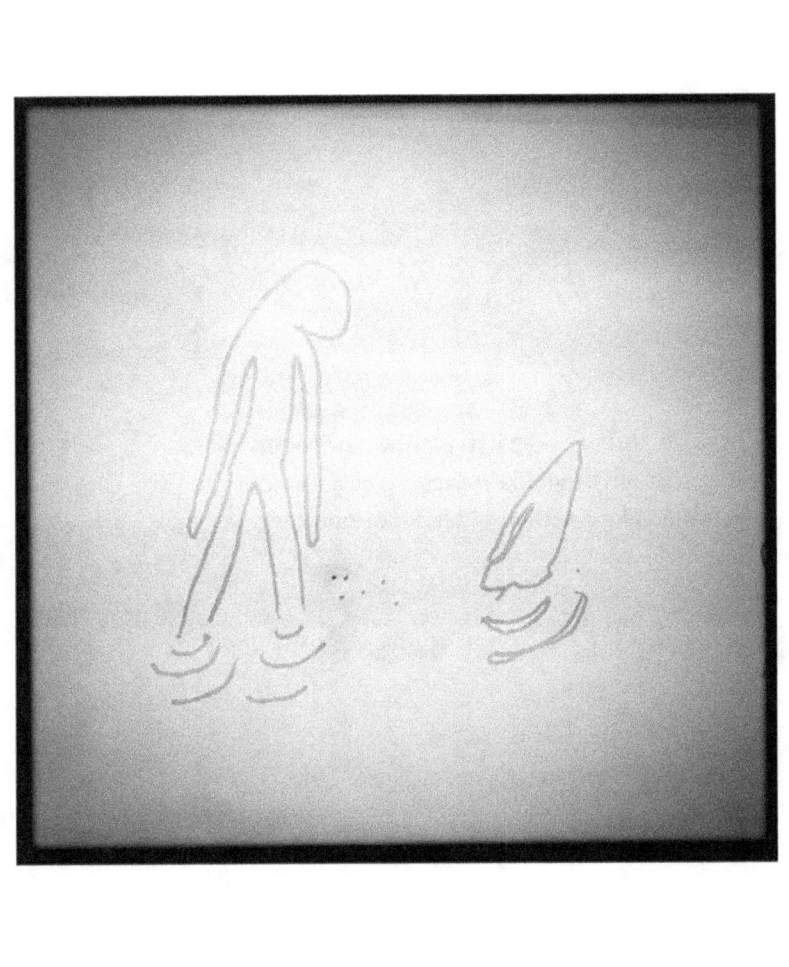

All of these letters make the sound
of dying, like a vacuum cleaner, collecting
like a withering black balloon.

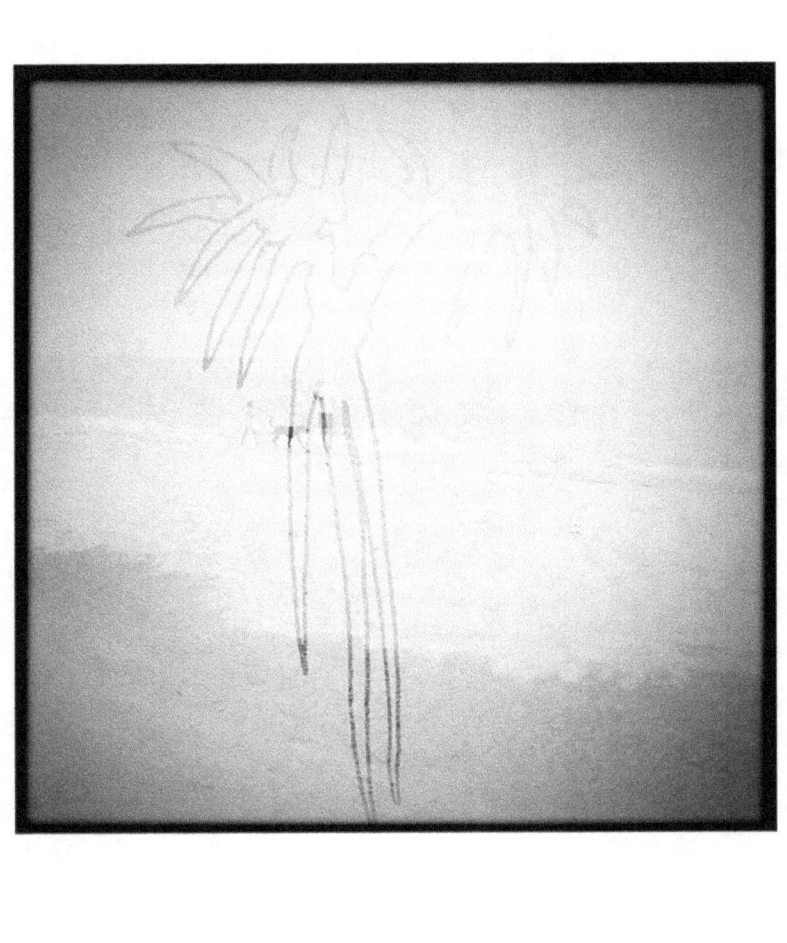

Here is the origin of matter,
so much easier to glisten.

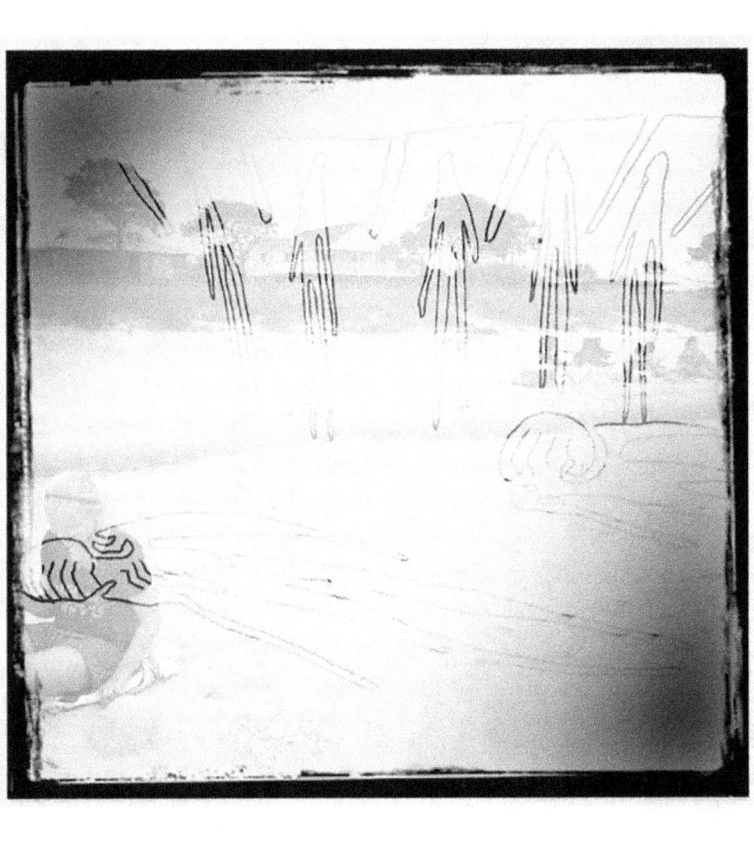

This body is a slowly crumpling envelope
as though in a flame or a fist
giving in to the pressure of bad news.

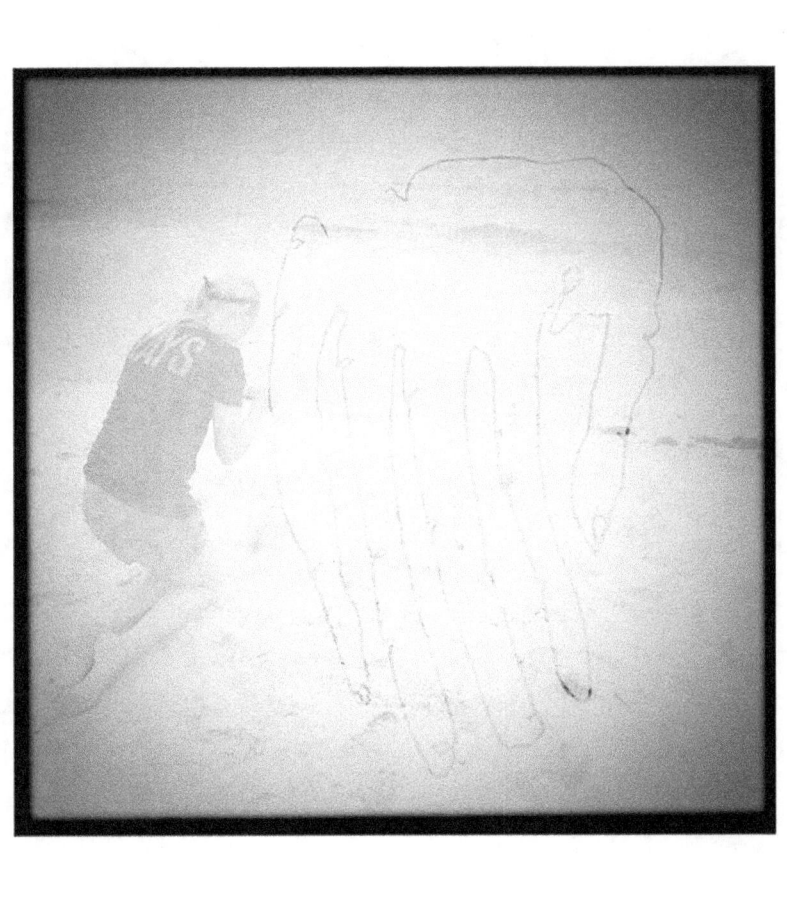

DENDRITES